Laying Off Employees

Pocket Mentor Series

The *Pocket Mentor* Series offers immediate solutions to common challenges managers face on the job every day. Each book in the series is packed with handy tools, self-tests, and real-life examples to help you identify your strengths and weaknesses and hone critical skills. Whether you're at your desk, in a meeting, or on the road, these portable guides enable you to tackle the daily demands of your work with greater speed, savvy, and effectiveness.

Books in the series:

Becoming a New Manager	*Leading People*
Coaching People	*Leading Teams*
Creating a Business Plan	*Making Decisions*
Delegating Work	*Managing Crises*
Developing Employees	*Managing Difficult*
Dismissing an Employee	*Interactions*
Executing Innovation	*Managing Diversity*
Executing Strategy	*Managing Projects*
Giving Feedback	*Managing Stress*
Giving Presentations	*Managing Time*
Hiring an Employee	*Managing Up*
Laying Off Employees	*Negotiating Outcomes*

Laying Off Employees

Expert Solutions to Everyday Challenges

Harvard Business Press

Boston, Massachusetts

Library of Congress Cataloging-in-Publication Data

Laying off employees : expert solutions to everyday challenges.
        p. cm. — (Pocket mentor series)
    Includes bibliographical references.
    ISBN 978-1-4221-2968-5 (pbk.)
    1. Downsizing of organizations. 2.   Layoff systems. 3.   Employees—Dismissal of.
I. Harvard Business School. Press.
    HD58.85.L39 2009
    658.3'134—dc22

                                                              2009019388

Contents

Tips and Tools   63

Mentors' Message: Why Handling Layoffs Effectively Is Important

If you're like most managers, you dread the prospect of having to lay off employees—and with good reason. This can be one of the most difficult and painful tasks in any manager's life and in any company's history. In fact, the heightened emotions, serious implications, and other concerns associated with layoffs can be so complex and intense that many managers conduct them poorly or avoid them altogether.

Unfortunately, layoffs are facts of organizational life, especially during volatile economic times. Managers who shy away from learning about layoffs risk handling them badly. And a poorly handled layoff is costly: it can permanently damage your reputation and professional self-esteem as well as corrode your company's reputation in its industry, making it harder for the company to attract and retain talented employees later. It can also lead to lawsuits, destroy trust and morale throughout the organization, and prompt high performers who know they're very marketable to leave the company.

Given these costs, it's vital that you prepare yourself to handle layoffs effectively, should the occasion arise in your company. The more you know about layoffs, the better prepared you'll be. This book will help. You'll find information and tools for handling the toughest aspects of layoffs, including how to clarify the reasoning behind a layoff, decide whom to lay off, communicate the news to employees, and keep your team productive after a layoff.

Layoffs will never be easy. But by learning how to handle them effectively, you help boost the odds that your organization will survive and achieve its goals after a layoff.

Susan Alvey, Mentor

Susan Alvey is an executive coach and leadership development consultant. She works closely with corporate executives to ensure that their leadership approaches support their business strategy and that their leadership behaviors are aligned to optimize results.

She teaches leadership courses in Babson College's MBA program and coaches executives through Harvard Business School Executive Education. She also serves as a Marshall Goldsmith Partners executive coach. Susan led the learning and development efforts for Harvard Business Publishing from 2001 until 2006. She continues to work with HBP corporate clients to develop and deliver on-site and online leadership development programs.

Steve Robbins, Mentor

Steve Robbins is president of Leadership Decisionworks, Inc., a leadership training and consulting firm that helps top managers become more powerful leaders. He cofounded FTP Software, worked as COO of BuildingBlocks Interactive, and, after graduating from Harvard Business School, codesigned the school's "Foundations" module as part of the Leadership and Learning project. Steve writes a monthly column for *Harvard Business School Working Knowledge*, has been published in *Harvard Business Review*, and has appeared as an expert commentator on CNNfn and weekly on the nationally syndicated radio show, *Entrepreneurs: Living the American Dream*.

Laying Off Employees: The Basics

What Is a Layoff?

We hear the term *layoff* frequently at work and on the news. But what exactly does it mean? Who decides to have a layoff? When does it happen? And in what industries? Finally, how effective are layoffs in enabling organizations to reach their goals? These are all good questions, and in the pages that follow, we'll examine some of the answers.

Defining the term

A *layoff* is a reduction in staff to meet a company's strategic needs or financial challenges. The reasons behind a layoff are strategic: the company faces an organizational or financial crisis that necessitates drastic action. The decision to lay off workers stems from upper management, but it is you, as a manager, who often must ensure implementation of the layoff.

Layoffs are never easy. Negative emotions inevitably accompany them, and these feelings affect everyone—both the employees who are laid off and those who remain. The company must take steps to avoid discrimination suits or other legal actions.

As hard as it is to experience a layoff, the challenge does not end with its completion. Layoffs will not revive an ailing company unless they are coupled with fundamental changes.

It was the hardest thing I ever had to do.

—A manager

Understanding layoff terminology

In the United States at least, the meaning of the word *layoff* has changed somewhat. In the past, both companies and employees saw employment relationships as long term: many people expected to work their entire lives for the same firm. Thus, most companies that had layoffs typically expected to be able to rehire the workers once the company's circumstances improved. Employees, too, often thought of layoffs as temporary.

These assumptions have given way to new realities. Employees today change jobs far more frequently than before, and companies commonly use layoffs to cut costs or to change strategic direction rather than to manage a seasonal workforce. Moreover, employees are accepting more responsibility for managing their own careers. And because companies no longer feel obligated to provide lifetime employment, they may view a layoff as a permanent loss of those employees.

Also, a number of other terms have cropped up that may mean the same thing as *layoff*. Examples include *letting employees go, downsizing,* and *rightsizing.* Terms may also vary by country. In the United Kingdom, for example, layoffs are called *redundancies.*

Because many of these alternative terms have become euphemisms for the blunter term *layoff,* they can damage morale and erode upper management's credibility. After all, those being "rightsized" know they're being laid off. And companies that use euphemisms can appear to be evading responsibility for the poor planning that led to the need for layoffs.

For all these reasons, we'll use the term *layoff* throughout this book.

Disclaimer: This book refers to some of the legal concerns involved in making and communicating the decision to lay off an employee. It is not intended as legal advice. You should consult with legal counsel who can advise you on the specifics of your situation.

Clarifying the who, what, when, and where of layoffs

Let's take a closer look at the details regarding layoffs:

- **Who decides to have a layoff?** Upper management makes the decision to have a layoff, generally with approval of the board of directors. Your supervisor may tell you that a certain percentage of your team or department must be laid off, or may identify which individuals must go. But in either case, you're the one who has to break the news to the affected individuals.

- **What emotions are associated with layoffs?** Layoffs are emotionally painful for everyone involved. It is certainly difficult for affected employees, but executives, managers, and remaining employees all may experience grief, anger, and fear. Managers who must conduct a layoff, as well as workers who survive one, may feel a deep sense of guilt as they watch former coworkers leave the company. Because layoffs solve only part of a company's problems, the response to a layoff is usually negative.

- **What are the legal implications of layoffs?** The company must be aware of numerous legal concerns. For example, if it lays off older people only, or all the laid-off employees happen to be women or members of a minority group, the firm may open itself to discrimination suits. If a termination for poor performance is disguised as a layoff, an employee may have legal claims that the company did not follow required procedures.

- **When do layoffs occur?** Layoffs occur when a company decides that it must make staff reductions to meet strategic needs or financial challenges. For example, the company must reduce its workforce, or it decides to eliminate a certain functional area. Most companies use layoffs as a last resort.

- **Where do they occur?** Staff reductions can occur in any firm and in any industry, and can range from dismissing a few employees to laying off thousands. Layoff regulations vary widely across countries. In some nations, companies can lay off employees relatively easily; in others, legal constraints may make it virtually impossible to have a layoff.

Acknowledging layoffs' limited usefulness

Often, people assume that layoffs will completely solve the company's financial problems. But while a layoff *can* buy a firm some financial "breathing room," if it's not accompanied by structural, competitive, or strategic changes, it won't likely revive an ailing company. And once a company has undergone three and four rounds of layoffs, managers, employees, and outside observers begin to expect the firm to go under.

Why should managers care about these patterns? After a layoff, they need to take steps to ensure that whoever survives the staff reduction can turn the business around and help it regain its competitive edge.

Before you proceed to the next sections of this book, review the table "Dos and Don'ts for Laying Off Employees." We'll be taking a closer look at the various items in these lists as we progress through the book. Use this list as a quick reminder of what you should do or not do as part of the process. You can also add specific policies and practices within your company to this list, as well as tips you learn from the experience of having to lay off employees.

Dos and don'ts for laying off employees

Do . . .	Don't . . .
Do think about laying off positions, and not people.	Don't just make cuts by percentage only without considering a more strategic approach.
Do understand the company's strategic reason for the layoff and its plans for the future.	Don't view a layoff just as a means to get rid of "problem" employees.
Do recognize that layoffs are emotionally painful.	Don't use a layoff to get rid of direct reports you dislike personally.
Do follow company policies and procedures, and get preparation advice, support, and/or training for how to conduct or communicate the layoff.	Don't delegate layoff conversations to the human resources department or your supervisor.
Do rehearse what you will say in layoff meetings.	Don't get pulled into a discussion about why a particular employee was selected.

Do . . .	Don't . . .
Do deliver the news yourself.	Don't mistake survivors' initial negativity as a permanent point of view. It may just be part of their initial adjustment.
Do communicate your support for the company. communication with members	Don't underestimate the importance of continued, clear of your group after the layoff.
Do be as honest as you can about the short- and long-term prospects for the company.	Don't forget about the needs of survivors; a layoff isn't over in a day.
Do explain that layoff decisions are based on company strategy, and not individual performance.	
Do deliver the news early in the week, if possible.	
Do refer people to outplacement or other resources.	
Do address employees' rights and benefits.	
Do allow each person time to react to the news.	
Do make exit and communication plans for employees' belongings, voicemail, and email.	
Do show your appreciation for the contribution that each person has made to the company.	
Do develop a plan for the future and engage the survivors in it; ask for their commitment.	

Taking Care
of Yourself
During a Layoff

A key aspect of managing a layoff effectively is making sure you yourself don't fall apart emotionally and physically from the stress and pain of the event. It's not selfish; it's making sure that you maintain the capacity to keep leading your team through a difficult time. In the pages that follow, we'll discuss some strategies for taking care of yourself during a layoff, so you can implement it effectively and help others in your organization navigate the transition.

Articulating the emotional impact

If you find yourself in a layoff situation, begin by dealing with your own reactions and emotions. Perhaps the most important thing you can do for yourself when contemplating a layoff is to *acknowledge* the feelings you have about the difficult task facing you. After the initial shock of the news wears off, you may feel one or more of the following emotions:

- **Sadness** over having to lose people whom you like, appreciate, and have known for years.

- **Guilt** because you're about to lay off people who have families to raise and bills to pay, and who take enormous pride in their work.

- **Fear** that you may lose your own job if the company conducts additional rounds of layoffs.

- **Anxiety** over the company's future.

- **Confusion** over whether you should leave the company in search of a more secure job elsewhere.

- **Cynicism** or **embarrassment** about working for an ailing company.

- **Resentment** that all the hard work you've put into the company may amount to nothing.

You may also feel some uncertainty and anxiety over:

- How to decide whom to lay off.

- How and when to break the news to the affected employees.

- How to prevent a collapse of morale and trust among remaining employees.

- How to realign work roles, systems, and processes in your team or department after the layoff so your group can support the company's needs as effectively as possible, given a smaller staff.

By anticipating and articulating your own emotions, you'll put yourself in a much stronger position to manage them and to help the affected employees and the layoff survivors navigate through all stages of the experience.

What Would YOU Do?

Bad News at BigCo

A T BigCo, SENIOR MANAGEMENT had notified department heads throughout the company that due to poor earnings and a waning economy, there would have to be a reduction in staff. "There are rough seas out there, and this is the only way we can keep the company afloat," Sergio's boss said to him.

Sergio was told that he would have to lay off Brad and Jelena from his group. He was horrified. Brad and Jelena were smart, talented, and highly productive employees. Why were *they* being laid off? Furthermore, Sergio was told he would have to break the news to them. Why *him*? He was their manager, but it wasn't his decision to lay them off. Someone from human resources, he thought, should tell them. Sergio dreaded Monday, when the announcements would be made. He wondered how he would handle the difficult tasks facing him that day.

What would YOU do? The mentors will suggest a solution in *What You COULD Do.*

Managing the feelings

To ensure that you're in as strong a position as possible emotionally to help yourself, others, and your company during this challenging time, try to do the following:

- Acknowledge that these feelings and this emotional strain are totally normal and appropriate.

- Understand that the layoff is not going to solve the company's entire problem. Rather, it's a partial step in a much longer process of reshaping strategy, enacting major change, and finding new ways to stay competitive.

- Realize that a layoff can create a profound and complex feeling of loss for everyone involved. Many managers and employees who have been through this experience describe it as a loss of innocence.

- Know that grief is a process. Often, it unfolds according to predictable patterns. For example, many people initially experience anger or denial. Over time, those feelings turn to deep sadness or despair, then to resignation or helplessness, and finally to acceptance. Whichever stage you're in at the moment, understand that, like most people, you'll eventually move forward through the grieving process and arrive at acceptance.

- Use your support network—family members, friends, colleagues, and others who are good listeners and care about you. These individuals can offer support and practical advice for navigating through the many stresses associated with layoffs.

Maintaining your health

Your mind can't function during a layoff if you don't take care of your physical health. To that end:

- **Eat healthfully.** Eat a balanced diet. Avoid junk food, alcohol, and coffee.

- **Exercise often.** Keep yourself in the best physical shape possible. Regular exercise can reduce your level of stress.

- **Get enough sleep.** If you let stress prevent you from sleeping, you'll only run yourself ragged more quickly. Get enough sleep and take time during the workday to relax. You'll give yourself the best chance of performing well.

Reviewing your job security

Before starting the layoff process, take time to address the possibility that you may lose your own job in the near future. In some companies, that fear turns out to be well founded: your supervisor may inform you that you *will* be laid off after you finish implementing the current round of staff cuts.

To protect yourself as much as possible in either case, practice tried-and-true career management strategies. Here are just a few examples:

- **Network.** Make networking a disciplined, regular part of your work life. Schedule networking phone calls and nurture your web of professional contacts through face-to-face get-togethers and online interactions. Make use of the online professional-networking sites now available. Your contacts may include previous employers, fellow members of professional associations, former colleagues, and so forth. But remember important networking protocol: when contacting members of your professional and personal networks, always do so with offers of help first. Don't approach newly acquired acquaintances with requests for favors. Networking is all about giving first and getting second.

- **Raise your visibility.** Conduct your own public relations campaign by keeping a strong industry profile. For example, serve on for-profit boards in and outside your industry or volunteer for trade association committees.

- **Watch for exit signs.** If you're worried that you may be laid off but aren't certain, raise your own guard. Examine the position and assignment changes within the company: do they imply an end to your position? If so, ask your supervisor whether your position will continue or how it will change once this particular layoff is completed. Cultivate a strong relationship with a trusted adviser in the company who has "seen it all before" and who can keep you aware of prospective changes.

- **Do your job well until you leave.** Even if you know you will be laid off, *conduct the layoffs as if you were staying.* Your professionalism will serve as a model for the layoff survivors, who will need to pull together and perform if the company hopes to survive.

What You COULD Do

Remember Sergio's concern about how to communicate the layoff decisions to his team members on Monday?

Here's what the mentors suggest:

Sergio's feelings of sadness, confusion, and anxiety are common reactions to a layoff situation. Sergio should take the time to acknowledge and deal with the emotional impact that this news is having on him. Next, he should consult senior management and ask questions about why the layoff is taking place and how the layoff decisions were made. This will help him better understand the strategy underlying the layoffs, which he can then articulate to Brad and Jelena. As painful and difficult as this may be for Sergio, Brad and Jelena should hear the news from him, not from someone in human resources with whom they don't have an established relationship.

Understanding the Reasoning Behind a Layoff

You need to understand the reasons behind the layoffs so you can support your organization and lay the groundwork for carrying out complex tasks and decisions. A good first step is to ask your boss some questions that will help you talk more effectively with your team about the layoff and make smart decisions.

Asking for information

Questions for your boss may include the following, as well as any others that come to mind:

- What are the strategic reasons behind the layoffs?

- How wide-ranging are the layoffs? Will this round be the first of several, or is it a one-time round?

- What is the future of your department and projects? After the layoffs, will the company's structure change in such a way that your team will be reconfigured or merged with another group?

- What kind of outplacement and severance assistance will the company provide for employees who have been laid off?

- Is there a standard company statement or procedure that you should follow?

Your boss's responses to these questions will help you establish context in your own mind for the decision to have a layoff and will help you later when it's time to communicate the decision to your team.

Supporting your company

As difficult as you may find the layoff, it's important that you support the company and do nothing to undermine morale, the company's future prospects, or the success of the layoffs. That means:

- Maintaining a neutral demeanor.

- Refraining from negative talk or complaining.

- Presenting the company's strategy and reasoning as best you can without compromising your personal integrity.

- Being as honest as you can about the short- and long-term prospects of the company.

The nature of your company also makes a big difference in how you support the organization. For example, if you work in a large company, you should thoroughly familiarize yourself with your company's established procedures for implementing layoffs (what to say, when to say it, and so forth). The human resources and legal departments likely have documents outlining these procedures. Alternatively, your supervisor may provide you with such documents, which may even include a script specifying exactly what to say when you break the news to affected employees and when you can do so. Be sure to follow these procedures carefully to avoid a mishandled layoff.

If you work in a small company that lacks human resource and legal departments, the firm's upper management may have consulted external counsel for guidance on implementing a layoff. Follow your supervisor's instructions for handling the layoff properly.

If you own a small entrepreneurial firm, you would not only make the decision to implement a layoff, you might also be the one to carry it out. Or you may need to explain procedures to managers below you who will have to lay off one or more individuals. If you don't have an attorney on staff, consult external counsel regarding how to manage layoff logistics. Speak with an attorney who is experienced in employment law.

Establishing your priorities

Preparing for a layoff can be time consuming. To handle the layoff effectively, you'll need to let go of other things on your schedule. Think carefully about where you want to put your attention and your effort. The following activities are far better uses of your time than getting sidelined by other minutiae of the moment:

- Building your team's long-term capability.

- Putting in place structures (such as new teams or new ways of handling certain business processes) that will survive the layoffs.

- Doing whatever you can to ensure that the postlayoff change effort runs smoothly.

Deciding Whom
to Lay Off

T he decision has been made: your company is having a layoff, and the event will affect your team. If the decision regarding who is going to be laid off has been left up to you, how do you approach this task? The following suggestions can help.

Lay off work, not people

Many managers, when asked to implement a layoff in their department, use an across-the-board approach, for example, selecting the most recent hires as layoff targets. This kind of approach doesn't work. Why? It doesn't take into account the core resource needs of your department. Thus, you may end up having to hire temporary workers to handle now-vacant positions. Those temporary employees often become permanent, saddling you once again with excess personnel. Your goal is to find ways to eliminate excess staff *permanently* and *strategically.*

Think in terms of laying off work, not people. Scrutinize everyone's workload and reduce it to the essentials. Strip away any work that doesn't add value or support the firm's strategic direction. Keep only those people who perform the work that survives this evaluation process.

For example, a company with a fleet of ships equipped to perform both shallow-water and deep-sea research determined that, owing to high insurance and instrument costs, its deep-sea research was adding little value to the company's bottom line. Senior managers identified all work associated with deep-sea research, including submersible upkeep and operation and maintenance of deep-sea fish tanks. Then they decided to lay off all the people who had been performing that work and who were neither willing nor able to be redeployed into the company's core business: shallow-water research. The company could then focus its resources on a more sharply defined strategic direction.

Some companies disguise firings as layoffs. But firing and laying off are two very separate acts. If an employee is really a problem, owing to his or her behavior or performance, he or she should be fired according to your company's established legal procedures, not laid off.

Equally important, don't use a layoff to get rid of direct reports whom you dislike for personal reasons. You'll further muddy the strategic connection between what work gets done in your group and whether each person's role adds real value for the company.

By reducing your staff *strategically*, you build a more responsive and efficient group that can help carry your organization forward after the layoff.

Consider social and team dynamics

Your goal is to end up with a team that can perform at top capacity after a layoff. Therefore, recognize that some team members' most important contributions may take the form of keeping your team functioning well, as opposed to providing a key technical ability. Pay attention not only to the output each person delivers to your customers, but to each person's importance to the smooth functioning of the team. You may decide to keep some employees because of their social or team-dynamics skills, rather than their technical skill or industry knowledge.

Consult with legal counsel

A layoff decision that appears to disproportionately affect older workers, women, or minorities, in a particular unit or company-wide, may raise legal concerns. Check with your company's legal counsel to avoid problems.

Communicating a Layoff to Your Employees

Once you've learned that your company must have a layoff and once you've decided whom in your department will be laid off, how do you communicate these decisions to your staff? This task takes careful preparation and a deft touch. Here are some recommendations that can help.

Announcing the decision to your team

People know when bad news is afoot. The message comes through in the company's unclear goals, the decrease in resources committed to ongoing projects, ominous-looking closed-door meetings, grim or evasive expressions, and other subtle (and not so subtle) clues. Rumors begin to fly, and employees begin spinning dark fantasies about what's in store for them. When people lack real information about what's going on, these rumors or fantasies can become far more horrific—and destructive—than they need to be.

Once your company's upper management has made the decision to lay off employees and has given you the authority to inform your group, announce the impending layoff as far in advance as possible, whether the layoff is hours, weeks, or months away. That way, you give your team members as much time as possible to get used to the idea and to prepare themselves for the possible loss of jobs.

If you're worried that an early announcement will cause important high performers to leave your company, you're not alone.

This is a real risk. However, keep in mind that if your high performers are already thinking about leaving, they'll do so anyway as soon as the layoffs happen.

Framing the announcement effectively

How do you frame the announcement of a layoff? Apply these practices:

- Discuss and acknowledge the company's position, including its financial situation. Share all the market data and competitive information you have, so that your team gets as much of the "big picture" as possible. If you have little information about these matters, suggest to your supervisor that the company provide the details to the managers who will be laying off employees.

- Make it clear that you support the company's decision and that the core issue at hand is the survival of the company. Explain that the layoffs are part of the solution to saving as many jobs as possible and ensuring that the company can define a new, more successful direction.

- If the actual layoffs are months away, write a weekly memo to your group or hold a weekly meeting to openly answer questions and share all the information you have. People may not love the answers, but they'll gain a deeper understanding of the situation. The more information you provide, the fewer rumors and disaster fantasies will circulate through your group.

- If you do not know the answers to some of the questions you are asked, tell people that there are some things you do not know and that you will share with them any new information that you receive.

- If appropriate at your company, explore with your supervisor other options for reducing staff, such as natural attrition, voluntary retirements, and creative programs that let people leave the company while still remaining connected to it through new business arrangements. For example, some people may be willing or even eager to take pay cuts, move to part-time status, or work with the company on a freelance or contract basis.

Sharing information in a timely way builds trust, strength, and understanding among your group.

Informing the employees who will be laid off

Eventually, you will have to deliver the upsetting news to the employees you've decided to lay off. Your *purpose* in delivering this news is threefold: First, you want to ensure that each employee understands that the layoff is about company strategy, not employee performance. Second, you need to convey your caring and concern for the employee and reduce his or her pain as much as possible. And third, you must try to quickly turn each employee's attention to his or her future.

Your *desired results* are to help displaced workers preserve their self-esteem and to rejoin the workforce as quickly as possible. The key is to set the right tone at the outset and to treat each affected person with respect, dignity, and appreciation for what they have contributed to the company.

To make sure you conduct your layoffs with sensitivity, follow these guidelines:

- **Rehearse.** Role play with your manager or with an outside communications coach or neutral friend. Talking (or reading) about communication is completely different from *doing* it.

- **Don't delegate these conversations to the human resources department or to your own supervisor.** Most people are loyal first to their manager, then to their company. Respect that relationship and let the employee put closure to it by delivering the news yourself.

- **Deliver the news early in the week, not on a Friday afternoon.** This timing lets affected employees begin looking for new jobs immediately. For most people, being able to take action quickly after they've suffered a hardship accelerates the healing process.

- **Deliver the news to one employee at a time, in private:** In a calm, dignified tone, reiterate the reasons for the layoff that you explained earlier to your group (or explain them for the first time if the layoff is occurring immediately). If the employee asks, "Why me?" emphasize that all layoff decisions were based on company strategy and work roles, not individual performance.

- **Don't get pulled into a discussion about why a particular employee was selected to be laid off.** Your goal is to keep the conversation to a minimum length of time so that you can help each person move quickly to the company's outplacement services.

- **After delivering the news, give employees a few moments to react.** Some people will want to vent or cry. Others will need time to think. Still others will want facts and explanations. Allow each person the time he or she needs to reach a stable emotional keel. Then, get them thinking about their future, rather than the company's. Make sure your primary message is, "How can I help you make it through this transition?"

- **Show your appreciation for each person's contribution.** Thank individuals for what they've done for the company, and—if company policy allows—invite them to return after outplacement processing to clean out their desks. Personally accompany each person to the outplacement staff member who will handle his or her paperwork.

Of course, telling employees that they are being laid off will always be stressful. But by preparing for this difficult conversation, you can improve the odds of delivering the message effectively. "Steps for Preparing for a Stressful Conversation" offers some helpful ideas that you can use not only in announcing a layoff to your direct reports but in any conversation that feels distressing.

Some managers have found it useful to work with a communications coach to strengthen the skills needed to deliver news about a layoff and to deal with other difficult announcements. "Tips for Working with a Communications Coach" provides some ideas you may find useful if you decide to have such a coach.

Steps for Preparing for a Stressful Conversation

1. **Become aware of your vulnerabilities to difficult situations.**
   Assess them before initiating the difficult conversation. Consider three separate areas: (a) **Facts:** What are the vulnerabilities you feel about the facts involved in the situation? For example, which facts do you know and don't know? Separate hearsay from fact and opinion. Know what you are and are not prepared to discuss. (b) **Feelings:** What are your vulnerabilities with regard to emotion? These may be your emotional hot buttons or of the other person in the conversation. Ask yourself what you will be feeling and what the other person will be feeling. For example, are you particularly vulnerable to hostile emotions in another person? (c) **Identity:** What implications might this conversation have for your identity? For the identity of the person you're addressing? When people feel their identity is threatened, they have the strongest reactions. For example, do you feel that your own well-being will be violated by the conversation—that you'll be announcing an action that opposes your own morals or beliefs about what is right? Will your news cause your listener to feel that his or her identity is threatened? If so, you may want to take extra care not to make the employee feel attacked on a personal level, that is, you can criticize his or her behavior, but not who he or she is as a person.

2. **Know how to react to your vulnerabilities.** Anticipating your reactions to stressful conversations can help you adopt more

effective behavior. Self-awareness enables you to engage in stressful conversations in a way that serves your needs rather than panders to your feelings. For example, if you feel vulnerable to hostility in another person, decide how you react to it. Do you withdraw from the person? Escalate the hostility? Clam up? Apologize and agree to reconsider your decision? In honest terms, write down your typical reactions to your vulnerability.

3. **Select a neutral friend with whom to rehearse the stressful conversation.** Pick someone who doesn't have the same vulnerabilities as you. Ideally, select a friend who is a good listener and is honest but nonjudgmental. Of course, that person should also be trustworthy and able to maintain confidentiality.

4. **Explain the conversation's purpose to your friend.** Start with content. Tell your friend what you want to say to the employee, without worrying about your tone or exact words. Don't worry if you're timid, cavalier, aggressive, unorganized in your argument, and so forth. Just get the content of your message out in the open.

5. **Think about what you would say if you did not have the vulnerabilities you identified.** If necessary, repeatedly go over what you would say if you didn't have those vulnerabilities. Refine the words until they are as neutral as possible. Your friend can help you achieve the appropriate wording. (He or she won't be experiencing the emotional intensity that you do when you envision having the stressful conversation.)

6. **Write down the phrasing you came up with in step 5.** Get your friend's help in documenting the phrasing you settled on. That way, you won't forget the words later, during the actual conversation with your employee.

7. **Now refine your body language and tone of voice to match your phrasing.** With your friend, practice delivering the talk that you'll later have with your employee. Have your friend point out any body language—a gesture, your posture, a facial expression—that doesn't match your words in neutrality.

Studies show that if your words and body language are contradictory, your listener will pay more attention to your body language than your words. Practice making your body language as neutral as possible.

Nonneutral body language might include distracting or emotion-laden facial expressions, such as eyebrows skittering up and down, body posture that says "I don't want to deal with this," nervous snickers or throat clearing, and so forth.

Also practice speaking in a neutral voice. Many people (especially in Westernized cultures) are less aware of their voice tone than they are of their body language. Yet voice tone heavily conveys emotion. Practice intonations and listen carefully for sarcasm, distress, or any highly emotional message your voice may be sending. Practicing into a tape recorder can help.

Tips for Working with a Communications Coach

- Select the right coach. A good communications coach can be an internal employee or external consultant. He or she should understand your company's culture and employee issues, as well as know how to facilitate change and transition processes.
- Work on the right skills with your coach, such as communicating difficult news in a timely manner, tailoring your delivery style to the demands of the situation, avoiding unclear language, listening to employees' concerns and emotions, and conveying empathy and resolve simultaneously.
- Look to your coach for emotional support. A good communications coach can help you sort through the emotional complexities that often characterize such conversations. He or she can also help you maintain needed perspective and can replenish your energy just by listening.
- Work with your coach to expand and improve your communication skills, whether those skills involve dealing with your direct reports, holding more meetings, or conveying your agenda.

Helping Displaced Workers Afterward

Part of handling a layoff effectively is helping displaced workers navigate through the transition after they've been notified that they will lose their job. You can play a vital role in providing this assistance, as described in the following pages.

Offering severance packages

The goal of any company that is implementing a layoff should be to help displaced workers find new jobs as quickly as possible. Many companies give a lump-sum cash payment to displaced workers based on their length of service. Severance packages also frequently include extended health-care benefits and full vesting in any pension programs that the company has established.

Upper management normally determines these policies. However, if you believe that certain changes should be made, consult your supervisor about ways to recommend them.

Every displaced worker needs help.
—Donald S. Perkins

Providing outplacement and counseling services

Outplacement programs or centers focus on helping displaced workers develop a positive attitude and master the skills required to search for a new job. To that end, high-quality programs:

- Offer psychological counseling to help employees deal with the emotions associated with being laid off.

- Provide job-search counseling.

- Acquaint employees with the local job market, prevailing pay rates, support services, and resources available through the program and in the larger community.

- Guide employees through self-assessment, including skills testing, so that they and the program staff members understand their skills, aptitudes, interests, and goals.

- Help employees complete job applications and write effective résumés, cover letters, and interview follow-up letters.

- Show employees how to work the job market, that is, how to answer want ads, use employment agencies, and build networks of contacts.

- Assist employees in honing their interviewing and presentation skills.

A good outplacement program can be expensive; however, such programs are well worth the investment in the goodwill that they create among laid-off employees and survivors.

The best outplacement programs include transition centers to serve as program headquarters. These centers include meeting rooms, reference materials, and an administrative area containing computers, Internet access, copy machines, and other essentials to help laid-off employees in their job search. They may also have bulletin boards for posting job leads and other information as well as a phone area in which employees can make unrestricted long-distance calls, even to friends and relatives (which bolsters morale and might turn up job leads). Such centers should also be bright, clean, and comfortable, so employees enjoy spending time there.

Supporting employees' job-search efforts

You can help displaced employees in several ways. First, make suggestions: If you see opportunities to improve your company's outplacement program, discuss your suggestions with your supervisor. If you know of open positions in other companies where affected employees could make a valued contribution, let them know about these.

Second, encourage employee participation in the outplacement program. Personally invite employees to use all the available services. Point out that if they take advantage of the program, they'll demonstrate their willingness to work hard to navigate the transition to their new careers.

Also explain that the outplacement program will be an important source of strength and support during a difficult time. Indeed, many people who participate in these programs stay in touch with one another afterward and continue to exchange job leads, ideas, and emotional support long after the transition is over.

Third, support employees' job-search efforts. Send letters to employers who may be interested in hiring your former team members. If your company has a computerized job bank, feed into it any results from these efforts. Yes, you'll be feeling pressed for time, but keep the goal in mind: quickly finding your former employees new jobs. If your human resources department is already handling this, coordinate your efforts with theirs.

Conducting exit interviews

Suggest that the firm hire an outside company to conduct exit interviews with displaced workers, if your company doesn't already do so. The interviewers should explicitly ask departing employees, "How was the layoff handled?"

These interviews give employees another opportunity to vent their feelings, something that can further accelerate the healing process. Inviting employees' input may also help demonstrate respect for them, which can influence how they talk about your organization with potential new employees later on.

Equally essential, the employees will likely share insights and feedback during these sessions. Your company could use this feedback to make any necessary changes to the way it approaches layoffs or to affirm that it is already handling them skillfully and sensitively.

Managing Layoff Survivors

A fter your company has finished implementing its layoff, your central task is to focus on those employees who survived. They'll be struggling with a lot of different questions, doubts, and emotions, including fear, anger, and mistrust. You'll need to:

- Help survivors manage negative emotions and rebuild trust and optimism

- Secure survivors' commitment to the company's new direction

- Make survivors an integral part of the company's new strategy

Managing survivors after a layoff is primarily about managing change. Upper management will be defining a new direction and strategy for the company. You'll need to make changes in your own group—in systems, processes, work roles, and priorities—to rebuild morale and help your team support the company's efforts. By handling this stage effectively, you can build a high-performing team that can better support the company's newly defined direction. You, your team, and your company all benefit.

Layoff survivors are . . . the most critical factor in determining your company's success.

—Bob Nelson

Acknowledging survivors' questions, doubts, and emotions

As the table "Survivors' Questions" shows, survivors will have numerous questions and doubts immediately after a layoff. These concerns begin with employees' own roles, expand out to the team, and then spread to the company as a whole.

Survivors will be feeling one or more of the following emotions:

- **Fear** that they will lose their own jobs in another round of layoffs (especially if they've been laid off before)

- **Cynicism** about management's leadership abilities

- **Sadness** that their former colleagues have left

- **Guilt** because they survived the layoff while their former coworkers did not

- **Anger** if they feel the company acted unfairly

Survivors' questions

Questions about individual roles	Questions about the team	Questions about the company
• Will my job change? • Will I have to do my own job plus those of my ex-coworkers? • Will I be able to handle the work? • Do I still belong here?	• Will our team have to accomplish the same or more than we handled before? • Where do I fit in this new team configuration? • Will this team still be viable in the new organization? • Have our goals changed? • Will we have fewer resources than before?	• Can I believe in the company's new direction? • Will the rest of us be laid off after we ship the product/finish this project? • Is the company's future secure?

What Would YOU Do?

Hyperventilating at Hyperlink

IT WASN'T A SECRET—Hyperlink Software was going through a tough time. The last three business quarters had been dreadful. No one was buying the company's statistical software product. Revenues were dropping; expenses were creeping up. Members of the executive team couldn't ignore the realities any longer: a round of layoffs was needed. Top leaders held a meeting with the company's department directors and told them they had to cut 20 percent of their workforces.

Jerry, director of technology, had been at Hyperlink for over fifteen years, during which he steadily rose to his current position. He managed a staff of twenty-five people, most of whom were very talented and had also been at the company for years. He loved his job and was fond of the people he worked with.

Now Jerry was faced with the responsibility of making five cuts in his group. As he sat in his office with the door closed, he wondered how in the world he would decide which of his direct reports to lay off to meet the requirement mandated by senior management. Should he focus on poor performers? Lay off the most recent hires? The employees with the longest tenures? What criteria should he use? The more he struggled with these questions, the more anxious he felt.

What would YOU do? The mentors will suggest a solution in *What You COULD Do.*

Identifying survivor types

Experts have identified three categories of survivors, as shown in the table "Three Types of Layoff Survivors." Each group has unique characteristics and presents unique challenges:

Three types of layoff survivors

Type	Characteristics	Your challenge
"Foot out the door"	• Proactive, independent, and high performing • At most risk of leaving • Maintain their productivity while quietly seeking other career opportunities	Find ways to reengage them and recommit them to the organization
"Wait and see"	• Reactive and angry • Feel betrayed by the organization • Become less and less productive • Feed off each other's reactivity and anger	Stress their role in the company's future and their importance to its success
"Ride it out"	• Most likely to stay but least likely to meet new performance standards • Risk averse and in denial • Feel disconnected from the organization • Most prone to stress-related illnesses	Cut through their denial; disengage them from reliance on the past; help them become self-reliant and empowered

Survivor types affect each other in different ways. For example, "foot out the door" types may spawn resentment among "wait and see" and "ride it out" groups, since they are more apt to leave the organization in search of better opportunities. And "wait and see" types can frustrate the others with their reactive, openly angry stance. Retaining members of each group requires a different approach on your part, whether it's the need to redirect their energy, empower them, or regain their commitment.

Tip: Hold a meeting or gathering with survivors soon after a layoff to enable them to express their emotions and say goodbye to a lost way of life at the firm. By acknowledging such feelings, survivors may be able to move on more easily to (and emotionally commit to) the new journey that the company is embarking on.

It's equally important to discern whether *you* fall into any of these categories. If you do, your team members may have strong responses based on their perceptions of where you fit in. For example, "foot out the door" types who see their own manager as a "ride it out" type will likely conclude that the organization is passive and badly run.

Your best hope of successfully leading your new team through the coming period of change is to honestly examine your own feelings about staying with the company. Whether positive or negative, once you have acknowledged your feelings and have decided to stay, you'll be able to do your best to support the firm's new direction wholeheartedly. Your trust and confidence will likely spread to your team.

Securing survivors' commitment

Immediately after implementing a layoff, take steps to ease survivors' stress and uncertainties and begin securing their commitment to the company's new direction. First, hold a team meeting with survivors the day after the layoff specifically to address their uncertainties and their questions about their own roles, the team, and the company. Try not to misinterpret initial negativity as a permanent point of view. Remember that your employees have not had as much time to adjust to the reality of the layoff as you have. They may need a short adjustment period to deal with their emotions before moving forward.

Also, to begin rebuilding a high-performing team after a layoff, take action to stabilize your group's best performers. Follow these steps:

- **Identify your top performers and determine the value each brings to the company.** For example, is one team member particularly talented at generating innovative new-product ideas? Is another especially good at fostering positive and profitable relationships with customers? Is yet another particularly skilled at strengthening bonds between team members?

- **Sit down with each performer privately.** Express your confidence in the person, your desire to keep him or her on your team, and your vision for the group's and company's future, including what's in it for that person. But be careful about making promises you cannot keep.

- **Ask for each person's commitment.** Honest conversations, heartfelt expressions of confidence, and a picture of an inspiring future are more powerful motivators than any retention bonus. You might say something like: "We've made it through a difficult period. Now we need to move forward. I want you to take the lead in repositioning that product line. I'm here to help."

- **Ask each person some challenging questions to get them thinking about the future.** For example, ask, "What are some ways we can strengthen the team?" "How might we redefine the team's work roles?" "What are the key competencies we will need most in the months ahead?"

- **Invite top employees to serve as trainer-coaches for their peers.** This can help foster a sense of mutual support within your team.

Through these steps, you'll help your best performers become active participants in the upcoming change effort, rather than passive observers.

What You COULD Do

Remember Jerry's questions about how to decide which five of his direct reports to lay off?

Here's what the mentors suggest:

Whenever a layoff occurs, managers should think about laying off work, not laying off people. Jerry should scrutinize everyone's workload and reduce it to the essentials. And he needs to get rid of any layers of work that don't add value or don't support the company's strategic direction. At the same time, he should also consider the social dynamics of his team. Technical abilities are important, but so are interpersonal skills. He'll want to retain employees whose positions are absolutely essential to the work that needs to get done and who interact well with the team on an interpersonal level.

Jerry should definitely not target employees for layoff based on their performance or their tenure. If he used these criteria, he'd be laying off people, and he should be laying off by position and job responsibilities instead.

Leading Your Team
After a Layoff

To maintain your team's productivity after a layoff, you need to apply some crucial leadership skills. These include formulating a plan for going forward, delivering a compelling message about change, communicating continually, and applying lessons learned from the layoff experience.

Formulating a plan for going forward

Once you've addressed layoff survivors' emotions and stabilized key performers, it's time to lead your team through the change initiatives that will follow the layoff. Your company's upper management may have created a general postlayoff plan, based on the new direction that it has identified. For example, a pharmaceutical firm may decide to narrow its research and development focus to fewer product lines than before.

If a general plan exists, you and your team need to determine how you'll support it. Your plans should:

- Take into account the new configuration and reduced resources of your team

- Be well within the group's reach

- Address new trends in customers' needs and competitors' activities

- Challenge old ways of doing things, with an eye toward creative change

- Be based on values that your team can embrace.

- Reflect your team's ideas, suggestions, feedback, and active participation.

Given the reduction in personnel, you may need to abandon certain projects or give other efforts low priority. Don't expect survivors to be able to handle just as much (or more!) work than they handled when the team was fully staffed.

Delivering a compelling message about change

Soon after the layoff, hold a meeting in which you deliver a brief, compelling message that has these three components:

1. **The case for change.** Explain how the industry or economy has changed and why the company needed to respond. Walk employees through the company's financial position in extreme detail. Explain what the layoffs, as painful as they've been, have gained for the company, for example, another nine months of guaranteed survival. Present the layoff as a prelude to a new direction for your group and the company, a direction in which the company will have a clearly defined mission and an organizational structure consistent with its new philosophy. Show that you support this move and that you personally have faith in the company.

2. **The key elements of the change.** If the company has formulated a general plan for moving forward, present the rough outlines of the plan, for example, repositioning of product

lines or moving into new markets. Make clear the rationale behind the plan and the desired outcomes. Explain how the changes that you'll be proposing for your group will help support the company's new direction. If your organization has not yet formulated a general plan, explain what steps the company will be taking to do so. Also, clarify how decisions affecting individuals will be made. Stress that team members' strong performance and support for the company's new direction will strengthen its position and therefore limit their own vulnerability.

3. **A commitment to what will not change.** Find something about your company's past that you can personally appreciate and publicly revere; for example, the company may have a renowned ability to recover from hard times or provide helpful and valued products to consumers. By honoring past values and achievements, you'll inspire team members to commit to the changes necessary to sustain those attributes.

Your goal at this stage is to provide clear information, win your team's commitment, and shed as much light as possible on what will happen in the immediate future and how these changes will affect your group.

Tip: Identify key issues you'll need to address in the postlayoff change period, for instance, low morale, resistance to change, or concerns about the company's leadership or direction.

Communicating continually

Through constant, candid conversations, you keep the spirit of change alive in your team. To this end, hold regular meetings during which you:

- Repeat the key points about the change effort.

- Let people vent their feelings and ask questions.

- Deliver up-to-date information about the company's direction.

- Define measurable goals and clear milestones.

- Explore ideas for how to do things differently and better in your group.

- Let people know which ideas you've implemented, and how they've played out.

- Celebrate progress, small wins, and new behaviors.

Also hold frequent one-on-one conversations with team members to acknowledge their work and stress how essential they are to the company's future; see how they're interpreting your decisions, actions, and requests; and encourage them to participate in the change effort.

Moving forward after a layoff is challenging for everyone involved. But by rebuilding trust through constant and honest communication and enlisting survivors in the changes necessary to move the company forward, you can help survivors *and* the company recover and excel.

Learning from the experience

As with any new and difficult experience, it's valuable to spend some time after a layoff assessing what you've learned and achieved. Laying someone off, though highly stressful, offers opportunities for personal and professional growth. For example, you learn:

- How to manage your own and others' emotions.

- How to master challenging new tasks.

- What your strengths as a manager are.

- Where you can improve your skills.

After making it through a layoff, you may discover that you learned far more than you expected and that you handled the situation more skillfully than you ever anticipated. And if you feel dissatisfied with the way you dealt with any aspect of the process, you can objectively examine what went wrong and then use the resulting insights to do better next time if your organization must have another layoff.

In short, navigating through a staff reduction gives you valuable new opportunities to enhance your knowledge, your managerial skill, and your personal and professional integrity. Layoffs teach managers to broaden their view of this difficult, complex task in several key ways.

Consider the time horizon. Before experiencing a staff reduction for the first time, many team leaders see the layoff from a narrow perspective; that is, they focus only on the moment in which the actual staff reduction is implemented. But a layoff has a much longer time horizon. You need to take important steps and make vital decisions before, during, and after the "main event." For example, you have to decide which employees to let go, how to break the news to them, and how you'll restore survivors' morale and focus after their former colleagues have left. Thus, the specific act of laying off an employee is just one narrow portion of the spectrum of decisions and actions the process entails.

As with the time horizon, managers who implement a layoff for the first time also gain a broader "people horizon." That is, they realize that they must not only manage the impact of a staff reduction on directly affected employees, but must also manage the impact on themselves, the rest of their team, and the company as a whole. By better understanding the impact of a layoff, they will also be more careful to ensure that future open positions are aligned with the company's direction.

If you're dissatisfied with any aspect of your leadership before, during, and after a layoff, you can learn from the experience and put better strategies and systems in place for next time. Sometimes layoffs stem from poor planning and ineffective decision making that occurred long before the actual staff reduction. You may be able to help your company avoid additional layoffs by:

- Engaging in more focused strategic planning.

- Watching competitors more carefully.

- Managing cash more intelligently.

- Setting more prudent growth goals.

By skillfully implementing a layoff, you also help to preserve your organization's and team's integrity. That's because you help the company refocus its remaining resources on a more effective strategic direction.

Though layoffs can be only part of the solution to a company's problems, they may buy time for the organization to get back on its feet. And by allowing the company to keep operating, layoffs save jobs that otherwise would have been lost if the organization had gone out of business. In fact, investors often respond positively to a layoff.

Handled skillfully, a layoff can help you forge a stronger self, a stronger team, and a stronger company.

"Steps for Leading Postlayoff Change" summarizes actions you can take to manage this challenging aspect of layoffs.

Steps for Leading Postlayoff Change

1. **Address survivors' uncertainties and questions.** Immediately after the layoff, hold a team meeting in which you share as much information as you have about the company's plans and new direction. If you don't have all the details yet, say so, but do share all the information you have. Invite survivors to air all their concerns, questions, and feelings about what has happened and let them know you're listening.

2. **Stabilize key people.** Identify the top performers on your team who are most likely to help the group support the firm's new strategy. Meet separately with each person to express your appreciation for his or her contributions and skills, ask for commitment to the postlayoff change effort, and engage him or her in thinking about how to make the effort a success.

3. **Gain remaining team members' commitment to the change effort.** Engage people in the change effort by inviting and using their suggestions, ideas, and feedback to lay out a plan for your group to move forward. By participating in change, people feel a stronger sense of ownership in it and thus can commit emotionally to it.

4. **Formulate a plan for going forward.** Decide how your group can best support the company's new direction. Consider new structures, processes, systems, priorities, and work roles. Make sure the plan takes into account the reduced resources available in your group. Make it realistic, achievable, and focused.

5. **Keep the spirit of change alive.** Hold frequent team meetings during which your team can celebrate achievements, identify ways to do things better, revisit the vision, raise and resolve questions and concerns, and fine-tune new structures, processes, systems, and work roles.

Tips and Tools

Tools for Laying Off Employees

Layoff Preparation Checklist

Use this checklist to help you prepare for managing a layoff. You can add company-specific procedures or your own personal items to this list.

Have you ...?	Yes	No
1. Received information on the short- and long-term reasons for the layoff? How do they relate to the company's strategic plan?		
2. Explored other options for reducing staff—such as voluntary retirements, decreased hours, or extended vacations—in lieu of layoffs?		
3. Developed your own plan for managing the postlayoff situation in your department or group? For example, how will you reassign work to the remaining employees?		
4. Reviewed company policies and procedures, including prepared statements if they are available?		
5. Sought legal advice if you are unclear about what you can say or do, or if you will be selecting the people to be laid off?		
6. Asked about what kind of outplacement programs or severance packages the company will provide to assist those who are being laid off?		
7. Thought through how you will announce the layoff to your work group or others?		
8. Rehearsed what you are going to say?		
9. Recognized the emotional components for all those involved?		
10. Set aside an appropriate time and place to conduct one-on-one meetings with those being laid off?		
11. Made an exit plan for affected employees that covers retrieving their belongings, saying goodbye, setting up new e-mail or voice-mail procedures, determining who will escort employees from the building, and other necessary tasks?		
12. Made a communication plan to address what you will say pre- and postlayoff to survivors?		
13. Prepared yourself to answer potential questions from remaining employees?		
14. Been taking care of yourself and your own stress level and needs during the process?		

Self-Assessment on Managing a Layoff

*Use this tool to reflect upon how you managed a layoff. It can help you recognize
what you did well and what you could do better next time.
For each statement below, indicate on a scale of 1 to 5 how strongly you agree or disagree
with the statement. A "1" means "strongly disagree"; a "5" means "strongly agree."*

Statement	Rating Low 1	2	3	High 4	5
I received company information on policies and procedures.					
I requested coaching from human resources or others as needed on how to manage a layoff.					
I used appropriate procedures and prepared for the situation.					
I managed the administrative details efficiently, including the completion of necessary paperwork.					
I maintained a respectful, realistic attitude in communications with employees being laid off.					
I maintained a realistic but positive attitude with my remaining direct reports.					
I gave recognition and support to survivors and employees who were performing well.					
I managed the change process effectively and tried to deal openly with resistance to change.					
I addressed my employees' needs.					
I engaged my employees in layoff recovery by seeking their involvement and commitment for the future.					
I listened to employee concerns.					
I avoided making or suggesting promises that the company cannot meet.					
I set clear direction with my staff to focus them on work after the layoff.					

Test Yourself

This section offers ten multiple-choice questions to help you identify your baseline knowledge of the essentials of laying off employees. Answers to the questions are given at the end of the test.

1. A layoff is:

    a. An opportunity to let problem employees go as painlessly as possible.

    b. A reduction in staff to meet a company's strategic needs or financial challenges.

    c. An appropriate early solution to structural and managerial problems within an organization.

2. True or false: Layoffs usually solve a company's financial problems.

    a. True.

    b. False.

3. Why is it so important for managers to take care of their own emotional and physical health during a layoff?

    a. They need to be able to make key decisions and lead their teams through the changes following a layoff.

b. They need to make a good impression with their supervisors and thereby secure their own jobs.

c. They need to explore new job opportunities and secure a position within another organization.

4. You have to implement a layoff. What's the best way to decide which employees to lay off?

a. Lay off the least senior people in your group, as well as those team members who have intractable performance or behavior problems or who have complained about the company.

b. Identify which kinds of work add the most value to your team and which individuals best perform that work, then lay off employees who don't contribute value-adding work.

c. Find out from your supervisor what percentage of employees the company intends to lay off and then make across-the-board cuts within your team or department according to that percentage.

5. Which of the following does *not* constitute one of your most critical tasks after a layoff?

a. Working with your supervisor to create a new strategic plan for your group and dictating it to team members.

b. Creating a compelling vision of postlayoff change and winning your surviving team members' commitment to it.

c. Rebuilding morale, trust in the company's leadership, and optimism among your surviving team members.

6. Which of the following represents the most appropriate way of dealing with employees' intense emotions, concerns, and questions during a layoff?

a. Let employees vent intense negative emotions briefly after announcing the layoff, but then build morale by encouraging them to emphasize only their more positive feelings.

b. Give employees frequent opportunities to express all their emotions, concerns, questions, and doubts, no matter how intense, upsetting, or critical they turn out to be.

c. Discourage employees from expressing any intense negative emotions and concerns or posing critical questions, because negativity can damage the postlayoff change effort.

7. Which of the following does *not* represent a good way to enhance your own job security during a time of layoff?

a. Make networking a disciplined, regular part of your work life. Schedule networking phone calls and nurture your web of professional contacts.

b. Raise your visibility by keeping a strong industry profile, for example, by serving on for-profit boards in your industry or volunteering for trade association committees.

c. Assume that you will be laid off and make finding a new job your top priority as soon as you learn of the layoff and during its implementation.

8. What are your two most important goals when it comes time to communicate a layoff to an affected employee?

a. Explaining why the person was chosen to be laid off and preserving the employee's self-esteem.

b. Preserving the employee's self-esteem and helping him or her find a new job quickly.

c. Helping the employee find a new job quickly and preventing the person from overreacting emotionally.

9. Which of the following is *not* a key benefit of asking laid-off employees (during an exit interview) how the layoff was handled?

a. Asking laid-off employees how the layoff was handled lets them further vent their emotions, which helps accelerate the healing process.

b. Asking laid-off employees how the layoff was handled can generate valuable ideas for making improvements in the future.

c. Asking laid-off employees how the layoff was handled reduces the chances that they will sue the company for wrongful dismissal or discrimination.

10. Which of the following characteristics most accurately describe "foot out the door" layoff survivors?

a. Proactive, independent, high performing.

b. Reactive, angry, feeling betrayed by the firm.

c. Risk averse, in denial, feeling disconnected from the company.

Answers to test questions

1, b. Most companies use layoffs as a last resort to cut costs in order to meet strategic needs or financial challenges. Thus, layoffs have nothing to do with individual employee performance and should not be used to disguise a firing.

2, b. Often, people assume that layoffs will completely solve the company's financial problems. To be sure, layoffs can buy some financial "breathing room" for a firm. However, if a layoff is not accompanied by structural, competitive, or strategic changes, it won't likely revive an ailing company. Thus, managers need to take steps after a layoff to ensure that whoever survives the staff reduction can turn the business around and help it regain its competitive edge.

3, a. Many managers may feel selfish about taking care of themselves during a layoff. After all, they likely feel guilt, sadness, and many other intense emotions for having to lay off valued employees. But managers who let stress overwhelm them by neglecting their emotional and physical health end up unable to make important decisions and lead their team through the major changes that follow.

4, b. A good guideline is to lay off the work, not the individual. This approach makes the most strategic sense. After the layoff, your group will have fewer resources than before. Therefore, it's crucial that the kinds of work most essential to your team's performance be retained. Essential work may be process related (for example, "registering new patents"), skills related (for example, "mastering and using new technology quickly"), and social-dynamics related (for example, "forming strong bonds and enhancing mutual trust throughout the team").

5, a. Designing a new strategic plan and dictating it to your surviving team members is *not* a good idea after a layoff. You'll stand a much better chance of winning commitment to change and generating more energy for sustaining change by involving your team in the design and implementation of the new strategy. Besides gaining team members' active participation in the postlayoff change effort, managers must rebuild morale, trust, and optimism among survivors and win their commitment to a compelling new vision of the group's future.

6, b. Layoffs are highly emotional events for everyone involved. By acknowledging the wide range of feelings, concerns, and questions experienced by your employees through all stages of a layoff, you actually lay the groundwork for rebuilding a stronger team afterward. Allowing people to express their emotions makes it clear to them that you see them as human beings, not as chess pieces that can be moved around at will to satisfy the company's needs. When people feel valued in this way, they'll be more able to commit emotionally to the postlayoff change effort.

7, c. Making your own job search your top priority during a layoff is *not* a good way to enhance your own job security. That's because your supervisor and employees can perceive such behavior as unprofessional. Instead, you should conduct a layoff as if you were staying. When you take this approach, your professionalism serves as a model for the layoff survivors, who will need to pull together and perform if the company hopes to survive.

8, b. By preserving the person's self-esteem and helping him or her find a new job quickly, you make it clear that the layoff is about company strategy, not the person's performance. You also convey your caring and concern, ease the pain associated with the layoff, and turn the person's attention to his or her future. Thus you help the person move forward efficiently and positively.

9, c. Asking laid-off employees how the layoff was handled actually has no connection to whether they will perceive the decision as discriminatory or illegal. Thus, this is not a key benefit of posing this question during an exit interview. Rather, the key benefits are that employees can further vent their emotions, which helps accelerate the healing process, and that employees may offer valuable ideas that the company can use to make improvements in the future.

10, a. In addition to these characteristics, "foot out the door" types are most at risk of leaving the organization. Specifically, they maintain their productivity while quietly seeking other career opportunities. Your job is to find ways to reengage them and recommit them to the organization.

Key Terms

Defections. Departures of employees (usually marketable high performers) after a layoff.

Displaced employees. Laid-off employees.

Downsizing. A synonym for *layoff*.

Exempt employees. Salaried workers who are exempt from being paid overtime; companies and federal and state laws distinguish between exempt and nonexempt employees in determining layoff policies.

Exit interview. A meeting during which a laid-off employee candidly shares his or her concerns or complaints with a human resources staff member; can be used to identify areas for improvement within the company.

Layoff. A reduction in staff intended to address a companywide problem by cutting costs.

Letting [an employee] go. A euphemism for *layoff*; not advised.

Nonexempt employees. Hourly workers who may be paid overtime; companies and federal and state laws distinguish between exempt and nonexempt employees in determining layoff policies.

Outplacement program. A company-sponsored program that offers job-search services, skills training, job-search tools and equipment (e.g., phones, Internet access, and copy machines), personal and professional counseling, a job bank, and other resources to help laid-off employees find new jobs.

Redundancies. A synonym for *layoff* used in United Kingdom.

Reorganization. A euphemism for *layoff*; not advised unless a restructuring is actually not accompanied by layoffs.

Severance. A package consisting of pay and possibly benefits extended to laid-off employees to ease their financial hardship or to gain their agreement not to sue the company for wrongful dismissal.

Support network. The family, friends, colleagues, and helping professionals who can assist managers in navigating through a layoff; support-network members help by listening and by offering advice and moral support.

Frequently Asked Questions

What documentation am I required to give a laid-off employee?

Consult legal counsel to confirm what documentation you should provide. In general, documentation should be as brief as possible but may include details of continued benefits, severance, effective dates of termination and pay, and, possibly, a nondisclosure or noncompete agreement. The documentation should not contain explanations of the reasons for the layoff.

If I have to lay someone off, can I get someone else to deliver the news or can I do it by e-mail?

The short answer is: delivering this type of message, in person, is part of your job. As painful as delivering hard news is, it's much better to do it yourself, and in person. That's because people form relationships with their managers much more so than with their companies. By delivering hard news in person, you honor that relationship and the other person's humanity, and you help him or her achieve closure on the relationship. With closure, people find it much easier to move on.

Should I explain the rationale behind a layoff?

Don't get pulled into giving a lengthy explanation of why a particular employee was chosen to be laid off. Companies use many different processes to make this decision, and layoffs are rarely the fault of the affected employees. Thus, trying to explain the reason may only create confusion for workers.

Only if the decision rule was clear and strictly adhered to (for example, "last in, first out") should you attempt to explain the rationale. It's more important to direct the person's attention to outplacement services and other resources that will help him or her find a new job.

After laying off someone, how quickly should I focus that person's attention on the future?

When people are laid off, they often need a moment to process their emotions. When you deliver the news, give the affected employees time to vent and then to pull themselves together emotionally. Then direct their attention to next steps.

For some individuals, a difficult conversation is as much about feelings as it is about what's happening. If you ignore their emotions, you'll make it that much more difficult for them to get closure on the situation and move on. So, let people express themselves, but don't get drawn into debating the merits of your decision.

Should I usher people out immediately after their exit interview, or should I give them time to say goodbye to coworkers?

This is a tricky question when it comes to layoffs. The most appropriate answer will depend on what kind of culture your organization has. In an adversarial culture, laid-off employees who are allowed lengthy time with coworkers afterward may use the time to spread bitterness and engage in sabotage. In a more collaborative, trusting culture, the situation might be very different.

If you handle a layoff in a respectful, thoughtful way, the affected employees will be less likely to want to spread bitterness among coworkers or commit sabotage.

What should I do about e-mail and phone messages for employees who have been laid off?

If you're going to cancel affected employees' e-mail accounts and voice mail immediately after a layoff, make arrangements to forward any incoming messages to those employees for a designated amount of time.

Clearly, you need to make careful decisions regarding what kinds of communication channels you want to keep open, for how long, and in what respect. Balance concerns about what an abrupt communication cutoff may do to the company against any risks involved in forwarding messages to former workers for a time.

Of course, your organization may have policies in place regarding these questions, so be sure to check with your supervisor or human resources department to make sure you're following those regulations.

I just found out that my company is going to have a layoff one month from now. Should I tell my team members about it immediately or keep it to myself until the actual day of the layoffs?

It's probably best to follow whatever policy your company's upper management has defined. In publicly owned companies, there may be legal reasons to keep a layoff secret until the day of its implementation. Also, the earlier layoffs are announced, the sooner productivity will decline while people ponder whether they are going to lose their jobs.

However, in smaller, privately owned companies, you may have more freedom to communicate openly and early. Open communication offers several important benefits. It shows that you respect and trust your employees to handle the news, and it may inspire some individuals to come up with valuable ideas for addressing the company's problems.

In any event, it's actually very difficult to keep a layoff secret; people have a keen ability to sense tension and impending bad news. Communicating openly about the layoff lets you shape the message much more than you could if you let rumors run rampant. On the other hand, productivity may suffer if people become preoccupied with thoughts of losing their jobs.

To Learn More

Articles

Morgan, Nick. "The Three Toughest Presentations." *Harvard Management Communication Letter*, September 2001.

Inspiring survivors after a layoff is one of the most difficult jobs facing any manager. This article explains how to win survivors' commitment to a postlayoff change effort, including the presentation of an irresistible vision of a successful future and then enlisting employees' desire for that vision in designing a way to achieve it.

Peace, William H. "The Hard Work of Being a Soft Manager." *Harvard Business Review* OnPoint Enhanced Edition. Boston: Harvard Business School Publishing, 2001.

Soft management does not mean weak management, says William Peace in this article. It means candor, openness, and vulnerability, but it also means hard choices and responsible follow-up. It means taking the heat for difficult decisions and giving unhappy subordinates chances to unburden themselves at your expense.

Ribbink, Kim. "Communicating in the Aftermath." *Harvard Management Communication Letter*, June 2002.

To minimize long-term effects on employee morale, companies must handle layoffs carefully. Thoughtful, honest, and consistent communication during a restructuring is essential to avoiding unintended aftershocks and getting back to business quickly. This article examines the assumptions underlying the language of restructuring and offers tips on how to manage the strong emotions that accompany the process.

Robbins, Stever. "How to Communicate Layoffs." *Harvard Management Communication Letter*, July 2001.

Letting people go is an emotional event, not just for those being laid off but for those who remain. Of course, those who are let go need help with the transition to new employment. But the employees who survive the cutbacks also need reassurance about their own future and an understanding of the strategic goals behind the cuts. Includes a study of one company that created a positive experience for employees during a period of massive staffing cuts.

Weeks, Holly. "Taking the Stress Out of Stressful Conversations." *Harvard Business Review* OnPoint Enhanced Edition. Boston: Harvard Business School Publishing, March 2002.

Laying off an employee can be one of the most stressful conversations a manager can face. That's because such conversations are emotionally loaded. Weeks explains the emotional dynamics that take place in stressful conversations and emphasizes the importance of preparation before delivering painful news to an employee. She describes a method for identifying your vulnerabilities during stressful conversations and practicing more effective delivery styles and behaviors.

Books

Caplan, Gayle, and Mary Teese. *Survivors: How to Keep Your Best People on Board after Downsizing.* Palo Alto, CA: Davies Black Publishing, 1997.

This book highlights the importance of recognizing different kinds of layoff survivors—from "foot out the door" types to those who take a "wait and see" or a "ride it out" attitude. As Caplan and Teese explain, these different groups will respond to a layoff in highly diverse ways, presenting unique challenges for you, their manager. The authors describe how to identify which survivors fall into which groups and how to keep top performers on board during the difficult time that follows a layoff.

Stone, Douglas, Bruce Patton, and Sheila Heen. *Difficult Conversations: How to Discuss What Matters Most.* New York: Penguin Books, 1999.

Informing an employee that he or she is being laid off counts among the most difficult conversations a manager can face. This book explains how to keep a cool head in a wide range of difficult conversations, not only in the workplace but also in the other important areas of your life. The principles and practices described here can benefit you no matter what kind of difficult conversation you're facing.

Sources for Laying Off Employees

The following sources aided in development of this book:

Caplan, Gayle, and Mary Teese. *Survivors: How to Keep Your Best People on Board After Downsizing.* Palo Alto, CA: Davies Black Publishing, 1997.

Morgan, Nick. "The Three Toughest Presentations." *Harvard Management Communication Letter*, September 2001.

Perkins, Donald S. "What Can CEOs Do for Displaced Workers?" *Harvard Business Review*, November–December 1987.

Robbins, Stever. "How to Communicate Layoffs." *Harvard Management Communication Letter*, July 2001.

Train, Alan S. "The Case of the Downsizing Decision." *Harvard Business Review*, March–April 1991.

Weeks, Holly. "Taking the Stress Out of Stressful Conversations." *Harvard Business Review* OnPoint Enhanced Edition. Boston: Harvard Business School Publishing, 2002.

Wetlaufer, Suzy. "After the Layoffs, What Next?" *Harvard Business Review*, September–October 1998.

Notes

Notes

Notes

Notes

Notes

Notes

Notes

Notes

Notes

Notes

Notes

Notes

Notes

How to Order

Harvard Business School Press publications are available worldwide from your local bookseller or online retailer.

You can also call:
1-800-668-6780

Our product consultants are available to help you 8:00 a.m.–6:00 p.m., Monday–Friday, Eastern Time. Outside the U.S. and Canada, call: 617-783-7450.

Please call about special discounts for quantities greater than ten.

You can order online at:
www.HBSPress.org